HORSE

insights

Secrets of horse behaviour

PUBLISHED BY

HORSE&RIDER
m a g a z i n e

SPONSORED BY

First published in Great Britain in 1999
© **D J Murphy (Publishers) Ltd**

Editor: **Kate Austin**
Designer: **Jamie Powell**

Published by **HORSE&RIDER magazine**, D J Murphy (Publishers)
Ltd, Haslemere House, Lower Street, Haslemere, Surrey
GU27 2PE. Sponsored by **Baileys Horse Feeds**.

ISBN 0 9513707 2 3

Origination by **PPG Ltd**, Hilsea, Portsmouth.
Printed by **E T Heron**, The Bentall Complex, Colchester Road,
Heybridge, Maldon, Essex CM9 4NW.

Acknowledgements: Many thanks to **Dr Natalie Waran, Fliss
Gillott, Jane van Lennep, Susan McBane and Sylvia Loch** for
their fascinating insights into horse behaviour.

*A*s horse lovers, we cannot help but be fascinated by the way horses think, behave, act and react. Horse Insights from **HORSE&RIDER magazine** brings together some of the most interesting features of horse psychology. Written by authors who have many, many years of experience (both theoretical and practical) with horses, Horse Insights *is* not only a good read, but also a valuable tool in developing your understanding of and relationship with these beautiful animals.

Kate Austin

THE AUTHORS

Dr Natalie Waran is a lecturer in animal behaviour and welfare at the University of Edinburgh and is also the Director of the postgraduate Masters course in behaviour and welfare. Her main interest is horse behaviour and she writes for both scientific and consumer journals. She lives in Scotland with her family and various animals, including three Thoroughbred horses, and is a keen amateur competitor - when time allows!

Fliss Gillott started riding at the age of two and was brought up with horses which completely took over her family's farm. Fliss went through Pony Club and Riding Club activities and developed a lasting passion for dressage. She still teaches riding for a living, and is reading Psychology with the Open University.

Jane van Lennep (Fliss Gillott's sister) also started out on the family farm/riding school. After qualifying, Jane ran a training stud/livery for 21 years and now breeds and competes with Endurance Arabs. Jane's approach to horse management is an holistic one, and constantly refers to nature and natural methods. Jane has written two books, and she and Fliss have answered readers' equine problems in **HORSE&RIDER magazine** since 1983.

Susan McBane has written 38 books, edited two consumer magazines and still edits *Equine Behaviour,* the Equine Behaviour Forum's magazine. She teaches classical riding and is a Shiatsu for Horses practitioner. Susan McBane is always happy to talk to readers and can be contacted on 01772 786037.

Founder of the Lusitano Breed Society (1982) and The Classical Riding Club (1995), **Sylvia Loch** has 30 years of teaching experience. She specialises in the psychological traning of horse and rider and is a proponent of the classical seat. Today she continues to judge, lecture and teach all over the world as well as from her home in the Borders of Scotland.

CONTENTS

DO HORSES HAVE
'best friends'?

We hear a lot about horses having herd hierarchies and certain ones being dominant over others with a strict position order. So is it really possible for horses to have best friends on an equal partnership basis?

Horses which are good friends will spend plenty of time within each other's 'oval' of space.

Horses plainly can be seen to pal up with others, and often have one special friend. What attracts one horse to another as a friend is as mysterious as what attracts one person to another in human relationships.

It is easy to tell which horses are friends because they usually spend a lot of time well within each other's 'oval' of personal space. Horses have an area of roughly 4m or about 14ft all around them which they regard as 'their' space. They have no social hang-ups and will either walk or skitter pointedly away from or, conversely, boot out an intruder.

Best friends behave quite differently: they take liberties with each other which no other animal in the herd would dare take. They may

graze touching, usually shoulder to shoulder, and may eat happily from the same small patch of juicy grass or out of the same bucket. If one wanders too far away, the other will catch up and vice versa. If one wants to play and the other doesn't, the second horse will put up with all sorts of pushes, nips and bumps from his mate which he would not tolerate from another, familiar herd member.

People often separate best friends when it comes to stabling, fearing that two 'inseparable' horses cause trouble if one is needed for work and the other is not. It is felt that in these situations it is good for them to spend time apart so that they 'get used to it'.

In practice, horses spend far more time not working than working so this means that, if they are not stabled near each other, they are going to spend all their stabled time away from their friends rather than with them. This may comprise several or many hours, which is a completely unnatural situation and one which can cause them a good deal of distress which we may not recognise.

It is far better for their psychological contentment, and therefore their physical wellbeing, to stable friends next to each other or as near as possible where they can see and ideally smell each other, than to purposely upset them by separating them.

The way round the 'bonded buddies' syndrome is to strengthen the horses' bonds with their humans, as well, so that they feel secure in human company and come to know that they will always be reunited with their best horse friend. Firm, empathetic riding and handling, plus plenty of quality time doing things together which the horse enjoys (not always work), and the knowledge that the human will never hurt, confuse or distress the horse, makes for a strong horse/human relationship based on psychological security.

SMcB

Try to stable friends next to each other - they will benefit from this psychologically.

WHY DO HORSES
move their ears so much?

Horses' ears are always moving, picking up sounds, scanning the environment - horses can hear sounds of higher frequency than humans, and quieter sounds, too. Their ears have another role in that they tell us (and other horses of course!) a lot about the way they are feeling and where their attention is directed. Unlike certain other animals, whose ears are obscured by horns, horses' ears are highly visible, even from some distance.

So what can the different ear postures tell us about the emotional state of the animal when 'read' in conjunction with a horse's other expressions?

Pricked ears are a sign of alertness.

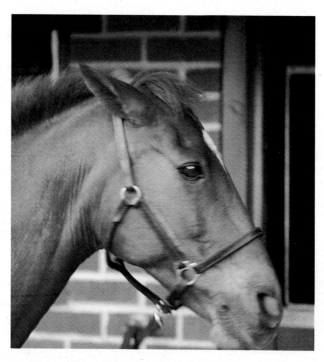

Pricked ears are an indication of being startled, vigilant, alert. To determine whether he is alert and looking for danger, or relaxed and simply interested in what is going on, look at the horse's body posture.

Pinned-back ears are, in the wild, usually considered to be a threat signal when two rival horses encounter one another, and are all about anger, aggression and dominance. And, as Desmond Morris in *Illustrated Horse Watching* (Ebury Press) explains, there's a practical reason for this: tucked back, the ears are less likely to be bitten or torn, so this helps keep the ears as safe as possible from the attacks of rivals. Although this is less relevant for the domestic horse, they have maintained this ear posture through evolution.

Pinned-back ears shouldn't always be taken as a sign of anger, however. Some horses will pin their ears back when they are plainly not cross - but more out of mischief, testing the handler's reaction. You can also see horses who know each other well and enjoy boisterous play, using the pinned-back ears approach in play. It may look rough, but isn't always!

Ears pointing in different ways show that the horse is splitting attention between two events. If you want to know what he is focusing on, follow the direction of the ears. Horses can turn their ears backwards, too, possibly when

Pinned-back ears usually indicate aggression.

- SEE THE DIFFERENCE

being ridden or trained and they are really concentrating on what the rider is asking them to do.

None of these postures are 100% definitive, but can be good indicators of mood and emotional state, and it is worth 'reading' the ear signals in conjunction with the horse's other physical expressions to work out how he is feeling.

KA

Ears pointing in different directions show that the horse is splitting its attention between two events.

WHY ARE HORSES
afraid of pigs?

Nearly all horses are afraid of pigs. However, when horses see pigs regularly, they are not bothered by them.

One reason, therefore, for horses to be afraid of pigs is unfamiliarity. Without the opportunity to see them all day every day, most horses are genuinely frightened by pigs, So, what is so scary? Indoor pigs are not seen, but they can certainly be smelled and heard, with their squeals at feed time making a deafening crescendo of discordant sound. That is enough to scare anything.

You see more outdoor pigs these days. Outdoor pigs are happy, cheerful creatures. Pigs are intelligent, inquisitive animals, and the sight of a horse being ridden up the bridleway next to their paddock is great excitement worthy of serious investigation. They will run squealing and grunting up to the fence, often scores of them at a time.

The sensible horse, perhaps not realising that the tiny, thin, low electric fence actually functions well as a barrier, will opt for out and try to flee. A heavy, fast moving animal like a pig crashing into the legs of a horse could easily knock it down, and the tusks of a mature boar could disable a horse by severing its tendons.

Outdoor pigs look frightening with their patches of wet mud. Their sheer numbers can be off-putting. And pigs love to bite on stones. A happy pig will have a mouthful of pebbles, which it gleefully munches and rattles - and which can be disconcerting to horses. And can any one say that pigs ever smell good?!

JVL

Horses which see pigs day in, day out, are not likely to be scared of them.

DO HORSES LIKE
being ridden?

Horses have been ridden for centuries and the easy answer to this question is that, surely, if they didn't like being ridden, they wouldn't put up with it! But it is not quite as simple as this...

This is a question which is going to become increasingly important over the next few decades. It is possible that the time will come when animal rights activists start to look at the whole concept of whether or not it is cruel to ride horses at all, particularly in competitive sports where, frankly, horses are at risk. The use of strong bits, martingales, whips and spurs to get the horse to submit to the will of the rider should be considered very carefully. To an outsider, it must, on occasions look very suspicious when strong tactics are used against the horse for the rider's pleasure and reward.

As riders and trainers, we really need to be able to see and believe that the horses we work really do enjoy themselves. Not only for our benefit, but also in a way that we can produce evidence for the uninitiated to demonstrate that this is the case.

To make a sweeping statement either way would be erroneous. Some enoy working, others most definitely do not. Anyone who has had a strong relationship with a horse will be able to tell you that some horses appear to love what they do and that, without enthusiasm for their work, no horse will perform well. It is impossible to force a horse to show jump or run in the National or complete a hundred mile endurance ride if he doesn't have his heart in what he is doing. The horse has the ultimate say.

That is not to say that horses must be enjoying every second of being ridden or they would refuse to be ridden at all! Many silently suffer no end of abuse because it is just about bearable. In this respect, horses suffer far more than cats and dogs for example, because of their silence. If they yelped every time the whip was misused or the rider was rough handed, we would all be far more sympathetic.

There are some very clear signals which the horse will give to let you

> Anyone who has a strong relationship with a horse will be able to tell you that some horses appear to love what they do.

know whether he is enjoying being ridden. If he is pleased to see you when you arrive on the yard, if he is happy to let you put the tack on, albeit allowing for a little teeth snapping at the girth on occasions, if he seems cheerful after work, then feel confident that your horse, at least, is happy. The horse which goes to the back of the box whenever someone comes towards him, or turns away at the sight of the bridle, is persistently difficult to catch even when left alone in the field, is not so happy.

It is worth remembering that being ridden should be just a part of the attention the horse gets from people. Grooming, handling and feeding are just as important. Horses love to be groomed in general, with many clearly enjoying the extra attention which goes with show preparation. Being well fed and well housed, kept warm in winter and coolly out of the flies in summer, are all rewards to the horse for being a riding horse. Without that one hour out of 24 when the 'normal' riding horse is earning his keep, horses would presumably be exposed to the elements and to disease and to the rule of nature which weeds out the weak and old.

There is much evidence to suggest that many horses thrive on the stress of competition. It may be the pampering, the novelty, the adoration of the crowds, the thrill of the adrenaline rush that goes with extreme activity. What is often the case is that a horse will actively seek the company of its rider after great exertion and become quite stressed if that person walks away. The horse which does not enjoy competition will be difficult to load, a bad traveller, lose weight when it knows a competition is in the offing and go seriously off its food during the competition season.

Stories abound of great equine competitors which become depressed after retirement and perk up considerably if they make public appearances as celebrities. Few horses or ponies seem to enjoy retirement after a busy life.

Horses benefit from regular exercise. With the security of a pampered lifestyle, they also have a need for sharp physical exertion from time to time, much in the same way as the office worker needs to exercise regularly as a stress-buster. Without a heart-pumping work-out to boost the circulation, the body will not stay in the condition in should be in. Being ridden should be one of the best ways to keep a horse's body fit and sound into old age, as long as it is combined with the right feeding and natural exercise at liberty with other horses. So yes, horses most certainly can enjoy being ridden and going to competitions. If this is not the case, there has to be a reason and we have to look to ourselves for the solution.

FG

There are usually clear signals which the horse will give you to let you know whether or not he's enjoying being ridden!

HOW WELL CAN
horses see?

Horses have a very wide field of vision, which is important to help them detect predators. But how clearly are they able to see things?

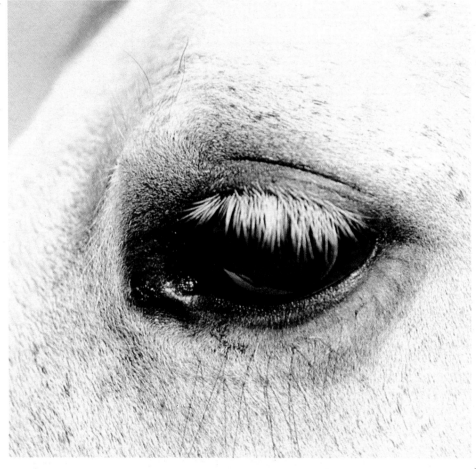

Relatively little is known scientifically about the visual abilities of horses. As a prey species their eyes are large and sited at either side of the head. This means that the horse can achieve a very wide visual field when its head is held high. It also means that the blind spot directly behind the horse coincides with the place normally occupied by a rider, and the blind spot directly in front of its nose ensures that it cannot see exactly what it is eating when it is actually eating! Horses have what is known as monocular vision - the ability to see separate views with each eye at the same time.

A wide field of vision has obvious survival advantages in terms of detecting predators and also for ensuring good visual contact with the rest of the herd. However this wide field of vision may be at the expense of visual acuity (clarity) at close ranges. The muscles around the optic lens of the horse are relatively weak, so horses use movements of the head and neck to improve the clarity of what they are looking at. This means that if the horse lowers its head, he can

see close objects in sharper view, but if he raises his head he can see well over long distances. The movements of the head appear to ensure that the image of an object falls on the most sensitive area of the retina, the visual streak.

This may explain why horses will often shy away from an object that appears to have been in their visual field for some time. It is likely that a change in head position may have resulted in the object suddenly being clearly visible, almost as if it appeared from nowhere. In addition, a horse's ability to see a particular stimulus will depend on factors such as breed, gait, training and state of arousal, since all of these are likely to influence head and neck carriage.

However, when an object is in focus it appears that the horse is extremely good at detecting very small detailed movements: much of its communication system relies on its ability to perceive very small changes in body posture, such as slight changes in the position of the ears.
NW

The blind spot directly behind the horse coincides with the place normally occupied by a rider.

CAN HORSES
get bored?

It's easy to get in to the same old routine in our own lives, and it can get a bit boring if you do. Can the same be said for horses, or is boredom not really a problem for them?

It is quite commonly accepted that horses can become bored. Stable vices such as weaving, box walking, crib-biting and wind-sucking are all said to stem from boredom. But what is boredom? My dictionary defines the verb 'to bore' as 'to tire or make weary by being dull, repetitious or uninteresting'. A weaving horse does not look tired or weary as it frantically swings to and fro across its stable doorway. Much of our interpretation of behaviour we put down to boredom is actually due to stress or even distress.

If boredom is not what horse people traditionally think it is, can genuine yawn-making boredom be ever applied to horses? It undoubtedly can, but it is not due to being stabled for long periods or condemned to solitary confinement when craving company. Genuine boredom can arise when the horse is only ever ridden in the arena, grinding over the same schooling exercises day after day. It becomes lethargic, lazy even, and always needs to be pushed on. That is nearer to the 'tired and weary due to being repetitious' of the dictionary definition!

The same horse, taken out for a hack, can suddenly become anything but tired and weary. The change of scenery will brighten it up and put back all the vigour that repetitious schoolwork bored out of it.

Horses, like people, will appear tired and weary if their lives are dull, uninteresting and repetitious. We all know of riding school horses which light up away from home, or riding horses which need stronger bits for hacking than schooling, or horses which jump brilliantly across country but cannot be bothered to do much in the school. That is boredom, pure and simple.

Distress and boredom must not be confused. A distressed, anxious horse needs its world put right. It needs comfort from company and routine. But the bored horse needs change and stimulus, some excitement in its life. Having plenty of turnout with their friends helps both bored and anxious horses. Their stables should be light and

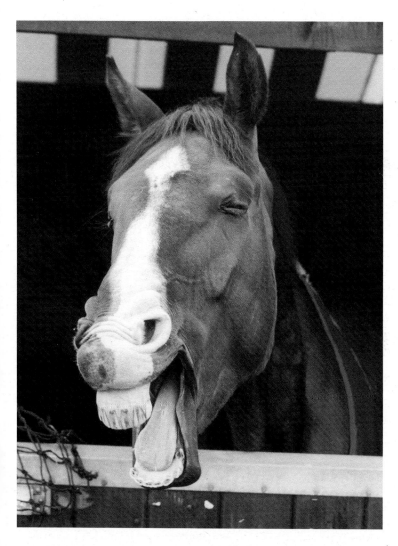

Horses can get bored, but we can reduce the likelihood of this happening with good management.

roomy; ideally with a grid between adjoining boxes so they can talk to each other and see one another without having to crane their necks over the door. Horses which can socialise are less likely to become either bored or distressed, and will be easier to care for and more rewarding to ride. They will be happier and, being under less stress, will be less likely to succumb to illnesses or disease. Perhaps we do not pay enough attention to our horse's mental health. It is just as important as their physical health, and directly affects it, too.

JVL

WHICH OF THEIR SENSES
do horses use to sense danger?

As prey animals, the ability of horses to sense and flee from danger is paramount to their survival. Horses put their senses to good use, but which ones are most important when danger is just around the corner?

Horses are supremely specialised and very efficient prey animals. They can get from stop to about 30 mph/48 kph in four seconds or less, all because of their amazingly efficient early warning system, their evolved highly-strung temperaments and a body structure that provides speed and stamina.

Because the eyes are well up the skull, the horse can see whilst grazing over most grass lengths to detect ground movement. Yet his view is hardly hampered at all by his thin legs.

The ears pick up sounds, with the large funnel-like pinna or outer ear directing the sound waves down inside the ears to the mechanism receiving them as vibrations. Because the ears can each turn almost 180 degrees independently and in any direction, this again gives more or less full coverage from wherever the sounds are coming.

Of the five senses (hearing, sight, smell, taste and touch), those used for detecting danger such as a predator (or anything perceived as danger such as a pram, umbrella or litter blowing in the field) are hearing, sight and smell - the latter only if the predator is foolish or inexperienced enough to approach upwind. Taste may be used to detect poisonous plants but is by no means foolproof in this respect. Touch is used mainly via the antennae whiskers around eyes and muzzle to detect objects in the dark on which the horse may bump his head, or via the feet to detect unsafe ground.

When a herd of horses is grazing they will always be calmly alert to their surroundings, and feral herds are known to post guards on the lookout for danger. Wild zebras seem to have a flight distance of about 25yds or 22m; they will let a known predator, assessing and testing a herd for a likely kill, get to that distance before seriously starting to run.

When a herd member, grazing or otherwise, sees a suspicious movement, hears an untoward sound or smells a carnivore, it will stop grazing, maybe with its head still down. Another herd-member nearby may notice this and, because horses communicate mainly by body language (position, posture and gesture), will think something is wrong and probably stop grazing, too. This alone alerts others, but if a suspicious horse swings up his head and looks, with eyes wide to pick up movement or shape, ears pricked to detect sound and nostrils flaring to smell an alien presence, others will certainly themselves note his physical messages and concentrate their senses in the same direction.

The original detective will probably be snorting by now, which will gee up any less-alert herd members. Within a very few seconds the whole herd will be milling around trying hard to discover just where and what is the danger.

Once its location is strongly suspected, even if the matter is not certain, the horses' speciality - lightning standing starts - comes into play, and the herd is off at top speed in the opposite direction.
SMcB

Horses are experts at lightning standing starts! They can go from stop to 30mph in four seconds or less.

- SEE THE DIFFERENCE

DO HORSES LIVE FOR THE PRESENT,
or do they worry about the future?

Horses are known to have good, long memories. Many of their reactions will depend on something that has happened in the past and the way we as their handlers have dealt with a particular situation.

Horses react in a particular way because they have come to expect a certain thing to happen through an association of ideas which often involves past memories. For example, out hacking, a particular hedge is remembered as spooky. At one time or another, a problem has been encountered here before. Depending upon the rider's reactions this time, the spookiness may decrease or increase. It is likely to get worse if, instead of soothing the horse and calmly riding past the object, the rider becomes tense or nervous themself. This does nothing to comfort the horse in the present situation since the rider is the herd leader, at least for the duration of the hack, and the horse is going to take his lead from that.

On the other hand, a horse may do something willingly like jumping, but accidentally he may clip the jump. If the rider punishes the horse, he may not associate this with the mistake but with the jump itself. This will tend to make him reluctant to jump that particular jump again. In all things, if there is a past unpleasant memory or sensation or pain associated with a particular task, it is unlikely that the horse is going to view similar future tasks with any real confidence or enjoyment.

I don't believe that a horse exactly worries about the future, but I do believe that he will become an anxious horse when there is no feeling of calm, safe and secure routine all around. This not only includes regular feeding and husbandry patterns but also patterns of a psychological nature. Predictable and comfortable owner/rider behaviour is vital to the well-being of every equine. Any irregular displays of aggression, anger, impatience, frustration, loudness or fault-finding will disturb the status quo.

Horses are sensitive creatures and thrive in a calm, certain environment. When they are punished time and again, and particularly when harsh treatment is exerted for something that is not their fault, they become very defensive as though always expecting the worst to

Horses need to feel that their environment is calm and safe.

happen. This influences their every waking hour so that a horse which is berated in its riding one day, may become uneasy and difficult in the stable the next.

Crib-biters, weavers, kickers and generally aggressive horses are more often than not the products of bad riding practices rather than anything else. This could involve anything from a badly-fitting saddle which nips the shoulder muscles and restricts movement, to poor riding posture. That is why it is so important for riders to learn not only a good seat which places the rider over the horse's centre of balance, but also the classical language of the correct aiding principles. Too many riders believe that they can ride on feel alone, but the great masters of riding have always insisted that practice without theory is insufficient to school a horse in a proper, humane fashion.

One of the biggest problems facing today's horses is that everyone says things a little differently wherever you go. There is no longer a universal, accepted method. One trainer does this, another does that. Horses come and go between different riders and different training systems. Remembered patterns in the horse's psyche may be swept away like crumbs under a carpet and yet the horse is expected to comply with whatever his latest rider is asking. It is all very difficult for horses when established goal posts are changed from day to day.

The horse has a very long memory. It must be excruciatingly difficult for horses that not only change hands and homes and all that goes with it, but when the training is changed too. We owe it to horses to understand his predicament so that the past, the present and the future are connected by a consistent, loving link.

SL

Predictable and comfortable owner/rider behaviour is vital to the well-being of every equine.

If the rider is comforting when something spooky appears, the chances are that the horse will respond accordingly.

CAN HORSES
see in the dark?

Horses are not nocturnal by nature, yet they do move around at night time. So how much are they able to see in poor light or in the dark?

The horse has good night vision due to the tapetum, which is a layer of cells that acts like a mirror, reflecting light back into the eye to allow the optical cells to use all the available light. In addition, the horse's retina is rich in rods, the cells that are most sensitive to dim light. Although horses are not nocturnal by nature, they are active for some of the night.

The importance of the ability to see in dim light is probably due to the importance of being able to detect ambushes by nocturnal predators, and for keeping the group together both at night and in dimly-lit habitats, such as those inhabited by some of the ancestors of the domestic horse.
NW

Horses have good night vision, which is useful to detect nocturnal predators.

DO HORSES
dream?

Unlike humans, horses do not enjoy one long stint of sleep, and do not need to lie down to sleep. However, there are some similarities in their sleeping patterns, and signs that they do, in fact, dream.

Anyone who has watched a horse lying flat out, fast asleep, twitching its legs and giving little whinnies, will be in no doubt that horses dream whilst sleeping. Foals spend more of their time asleep, so it can be easier to watch a foal, rather than a horse, enjoying a good dream.

Research into the sleeping patterns of domestic animals, including horses, reinforces this viewpoint. As Lesley Skipper in her excellent book, *Inside Your Horse's Mind* (J A Allen), explains: "Sleep falls into several categories, depending on the level of brain activity. Paradoxical or rapid eye movement (REM) is characterised by patterns of brain activity which indicate dreaming." However, it seems that REM sleep only occurs in horses who are lying flat. Indeed, it is thought that REM is essential to their mental health: animals deprived of REM sleep can suffer from severe psychological disturbances.

Although horses can sleep standing up, it is thought that they enjoy a better quality sleep if they can lie out flat.

It is unusual to see a whole herd of horses in the wild all lying down as this would make the herd more vulnerable to predators.

Horses are unusual in that they can sleep without lying down, due to their stay apparatus which enables them to stand upright without muscular effort. This mechanism has proved to be particularly useful for horses in the wild: it takes effort for such large animals to get up from lying down, which adds to their vulnerability if there are predators around. Hence, it is unusual to see a whole herd of horses in the wild all lying down. (In a secure domestic situation, it is perfectly normal to see all the horses in a group lying down together.) All horses, however, will lie down for an average of 10 per cent of their time if they are free to do so.

When we dream we often re-live previous experiences, and it seems that horses may do exactly the same as us. Many people have reported horses which have been in battle experiencing disturbed dreams afterwards. Perhaps we should all spend more time with our horses when they are sleeping to see how they react to the day's experiences when they 'go to bed' that night!

KA

HOW GOOD IS THE
horse's memory?

To make the most of the learning capabilities of horses, it is best to work with, rather than against, their natural behavioural traits and to understand that horses vary widely in their ability to learn.

The performance or sport horse is expected to perform a wide variety of tasks, all of which need to be learned and remembered. Training is therefore the process by which the human handler introduces the horse to new situations and associations. The horse is often required to accept practices it may find instinctively unpleasant or threatening, and to respond to unnatural stimuli such as leg pressure from a rider with often unnatural or over emphasised behaviour, such as the high school movements performed by dressage horses.

In order for the horse to learn properly and to retain information during training it must be motivated in some way. Often this is due to the close relationship that the trainer has developed with the horse through the training process, and the fact that horses appear to bond with humans, accepting praise in reward for the correct responses. Poor training methods, such as the misuse of punishment, lead to behavioural and welfare problems.

Foals that are handled intensively find it easier to cope with training and management later in life.

Recent research on the learning capabilities of horses encourages approaches to training that work with, rather than against, the natural behavioural traits of the horse. Scientific studies of the perceptive abilities of domestic horses help us understand the way in which horses learn, and can be used to help the training process.

It is obvious from such studies that horses vary widely in their ability to learn, and that opportunities to learn early in life help in the training process later. Highly emotional horses, and those who show the greatest fear responses in standard scientific tests, did less well in learning trials, and there is some evidence that breed differences also exist. Thoroughbreds apparently learn less well than Quarterhorses, perhaps due to their early developmental experiences. Learning ability also appears to decline with age. No relationship has been found between dominance status or sex in ability to learn. This is despite anecdotal reports that dominant horses can be difficult to train and are more likely to find a means of evading the trainer.

31

Orphan foals reared by humans are less emotional when placed in an unfamiliar environment compared with normally reared foals, which suggests that early handling can influence reactivity later in life. Robert Miller, a well known American vet and behaviourist, suggests the use of 'imprint training' for newly born foals. By intensively handling foals, he claims early bonding between human and horse takes place, which enhances the ability of the horse to cope with training and management later in life. This method of training does appear to fit with the natural behavioural traits of young horses in free living situations, who are constantly absorbing information during their time with the herd before reaching maturity at three years. Despite this information, most horses under typical domestic conditions are rarely intensively handled until they are considered sufficiently physically developed to carry a rider at about three years.

NW

CAN HORSES

cry?

Horses can certainly shed tears, but are they ever as a result of emotional upset, or are they simply a physical response to certain stimulii?

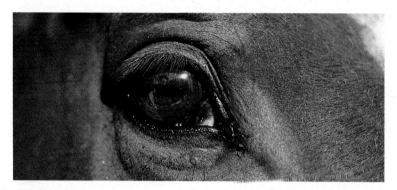

Anyone who has seen a horse with an eye infection or irritation that has caused conjunctivitis, is left in no doubt about the ability of horses to produce tears. Tears keep the eye moist and have an important function in maintaining the health of the eye.

However, there is no evidence that horses cry in the same way that humans do when in a particular emotional state. That is not to say that horses do not feel sadness, pain etc, but they probably express such feelings in a different way to the human species.

The eye itself, though, is often used as an indicator of the horse's emotional state. A rolling eye is often used to indicate an anxious state, and showing the white of the eye is often quoted as indicating a fearful horse or, if accompanied by an ear back motion, may be used to signal an aggressive attack. A very 'fixed' eye may be used to indicate the horse in pain, and horses with 'soft', watery eyes are often seen as calm and relaxed.

Of course there is little science to back this up, but most experienced horse people probably inadvertently use such signals in assessing a horse's temperament and attitude.
NW

WHY DO ALL THE HORSES IN A FIELD

prance around when a new-comer is introduced?

Horses will usually prance around - heads and tails raised, necks arched - when a new, strange horse enters their field. Horses do not like change and this behaviour is part of their instinctive reaction to seeing a new stranger entering their ranks.

There is always great excitement when a new horse is introduced to an established herd. The herd will already have sorted out some sort of pecking order and friendship grouping. They will know which horses are aggressive and are best avoided and which will keep out of the way with the slightest intimidation. A new horse is an unknown quantity. The established group will rally together excluding the stranger, which will only be allowed to the very fringe of the old herd. On occasions, this exclusion will become very aggressive and physical until the newcomer has learned to read the actions of the others and is able to take avoiding action without being hurt.

So why all the prancing and posturing? It is a form of showing off, a displaying of physical prowess. Elevated strides, raised heads and tails, arched necks and snorting - all these things combine to make the horse or pony look bigger, more impressive and more intimidating than usual. The 'ganging up' is part of utilising safety in numbers. Horses do not like change and will instinctively keep a stranger out of their ranks until it is ready to conform to their rules and fit in. Once accepted, usually at the bottom of the pecking order, the new horse

will start to assert itself and eventually fit in to its rightful natural place in the herd.

In mixed groups, the displaying is likely to last longer and be more aggressive in nature. Although geldings are not full-blooded males, they often retain a lot of their male instincts which includes having their own herd of females and guarding them from other males. A new male introduced to the herd will have a very hard time fitting in with the other males although the mares may well be very interested and vie for his attention.

A new mare may not be welcomed by the other mares but will cause much squabbling amongst the boys. There may then be posturing to the new mare in competition with each other. Bearing in mind that the bigger, faster and more powerful entire will be the one likely to win the greater number of mares in his sub-group, it is in his interests to look like the biggest, fastest and most powerful male present.

Horses will often prance around when a newcomer enters the field.

Interestingly, the showing off that takes place on such occasions is a wonderful opportunity to see the horse producing natural dressage. Every movement required at any of the levels may be shown by the horse at liberty when it wishes to impress, especially in a mixed sex group. Even little native ponies will show great collection, lateral work, piaffe, passage and airs above the ground in the right circumstances. If only we could get them to feel like showing off under saddle without losing control, dressage would be so easy!

FG

DO HORSES GET
jealous?

Horses are capable of being jealous and will show this in different ways. If we treat all the horses in our care fairly, without showing favouritism to one over another, we can help to keep feelings of jealousy to a minimum.

Horses are no different from any other domestic animal when it comes to petty jealousies, craving for attention and jostling for supremacy. Many horses really do want to be number one and will go out of their way to be so, particularly in a stable situation.

I have a mixed stable, where the horses look into a barn arrangement on one side and the great outdoors on the other. Whichever side you approach, all heads are quick to arrive over the door the moment voices are heard and one can note a definite degree of competitiveness as each individual does his best to be spoken to and admired first.

Some would argue that this response is stimulated by greed, but this is not the case. Often, no food is proffered, but this does not put the incumbents off. I have however noticed with some visiting horses, that no food means total switch-off. In such a case it would therefore appear that the animal concerned is not used to being fussed over, so there is no expectation of pleasurable feelings.

Like children, horses that are used to attention and praise will be anxious for more of the same. This may lead to real jealousy if it is seen that someone else is getting more than their fair share. I am constantly amazed when one reads articles about the behaviour of horses in the general press. Few non-horse people allow that a horse may have 'feelings' like a dog. Yet anyone who owns a horse must be well aware of his facial and postural expressions which are a clear indication of his state of mind and the emotions that rule his behaviour.

Jealousy is as definite an emotion for horses as it is for us but it may be shown in a number of different ways. Depending on the character of the horse, some of these reactions may be overt, aggressive and noisy; in others the horse shows his jealousy by turning his back and going all quiet and huffy. In my barn, the line-up of boxes contains the following: a gelding, a mare, another gelding, a very old stallion, and another old stallion in that order. The older stallion is the senior member of the stable and he simply will not talk to me for hours if he feels someone else has enjoyed more attention than he. He also becomes quite explosive to ride if he is not the first one of the day to be exercised. First out, however, he is always as good as gold.

The mare, who has also been with me a long time, does her very best to be noticed at all times. She flashes her eyes, flutters her lashes and expects to be touched first as she pokes her nose over the door in the most expectant and pushy way. If one does not comply, she is furious. She bangs the door and tosses her head with great impatience. She adores her friend next door and they can touch noses, but if he is being caressed before her, she bares her teeth at him, flattens her ears and bangs her door with much squealing. Once, however, she caught me with her teeth instead of him. Instantly, she was mortified and made it very plain how sorry she was, nuzzling me and breathing down her nostrils to show her abject apologies.

Whilst most of the horses enjoy being hacked out together, I am unable to ride one of the geldings out with the senior stallion. This is because the gelding is my competition horse and unlike the other horses, is not used for lessons. This infuriates the stallion who used to be my *numero uno* but who is now too old to travel. He often watches me schooling from the stable with a bitter look on his face, but we try to make it up to him in other ways. Nevertheless, I know that the stallion would gladly teach the gelding a lesson if he could, since on one terrible occasion they got out together and this very nearly happened. It was all down to jealousy.

SL

Depending on the character of the horse, jealousy may be demonstrated with aggressive behaviour.

DO HORSES ADJUST TO
living alone?

Horses have evolved in many different ways over the years, so is it possible for them to abandon their instinctive herd behaviour and adapt to solitary living?

Horses are naturally herd animals. They find security, society and comfort in their herd. Within the larger herd, there are often sub-divisions into small groups of friends or closely related individuals. The herd is largely female, with a stallion doing his best to keep his harem from being poached by other marauding stallions. Colts at puberty will be driven away, to form temporary groups of bachelor males. Once fully mature, these will in turn try to collect a herd of females, perhaps starting off with a young filly. Unsuccessful males will be left on their own, either because they are unable to prise any females away from another stallion, or because, due to old age and the inability to fight off a younger, stronger stallion, they have had all their mares poached away from them. In extreme old age, her herd might leave behind a mare, unable to keep up due to weakness or lameness.

These horses which end up on their own in the natural course of

Horses that are kept on their own need lots of extra attention.

events are doomed. On their own they are extremely vulnerable and will not survive for long. A solitary life is a death sentence for a horse in the wild.

Many unfortunate horses are kept on their own. It is important to accept that this is totally unnatural for a horse. A horse should not be expected to live on its own. On its own, it will inevitably have to make major adjustments and is likely to have some form of disturbed behaviour.

On its own, a horse may well develop a strong, even passionate, bond with another creature. One hears of racehorses which can go nowhere without their 'pet' hen or goat. They can become attached to a sheep or a cat. They need company. Without suitable equine companionship, the solitary horse will become more dependent on its human carers, which may seem very touching when it whinnies with excitement on your arrival at the field or stable, and stares sadly after you on your departure, but it is not really in the horse's best interests. When a lone horse does meet another horse, there is often huge excitement. It may whinny, pose, prance and show off. If it gets close to another horse, it may squeal, strike out or kick. Its behaviour can be very 'over the top' and it can take a long time to settle down again.

All horses benefit from being with others.

The lone horse will need lots of extra attention. When you are picking up droppings, for instance, it is likely to remain close. It will appreciate extra grooming, as it has no one else to scratch the itchy bits. Denied another horse to play with, young or boisterous horses can become difficult to handle and can try to dominate their humans. They will need firm, but sympathetic, handling and can benefit from discipline such as lungeing or long reining.

Older horses can appear to adapt better to solitary confinement than younger ones, but the truth is that any horse is happier if it can at least see and, hopefully, touch another. Without company, horses can become depressed, withdrawn and disturbed. Is it worth it?
JVL

WHY DO MARES
bite more than geldings when girthed up?

Mares are definitely ticklish around the girth area, and will let you know when you are tacking up and grooming what they think of it. There are good reasons for this behaviour, and it's all to do with being a mare.

Mares are generally much more sensitive than geldings around the girth and belly area, while colts, stallions and geldings are more likely than mares to object to having their front legs handled, especially if they are generally nervous. As there are clear gender differences, the explanation has to be to do with gender as well.

Stallions fight for supremacy by attacking the opposition's front legs. It is an effective way of bringing down the opponent. Hence 'boys' need to trust their handlers to allow them to handle this part of their anatomy.

A stallion attracted to a mare because she is coming in season will not approach the back end until he is sure he is right and she is receptive - otherwise he will get kicked! He is more likely to sidle up to the front and and nibble her around the withers, the girth and the belly. If she does not welcome his attentions, she will snap round at him. When she is receptive, she may find this sort of attention quite a 'turn on' and will swing her body into him - as long as his technique is just right.

Broadly speaking, the ticklish areas of a mare's body are her erogenous zones, but only when the time is right and the touch is right. Although some mares are capable of overcoming their more basic instincts and no longer view grooming and tacking up as any kind of erotic gesture, others remain tetchy to their dying days.

FG

WHY DOES A HORSE
lower its head at a drop fence?

There are plenty of theories and some good, practical reasons which explain why horses lower their heads on the approach to drop fences.

Below left: the classic posture on approach to a drop fence - lowered head, bending at the knees...

Horses' eyes are set wide on the side of the head to give good all-round vision. The price for this is that they do not focus well at close range in front. It is difficult to be certain how they compensate for this apparent weakness, particularly when it comes to jumping and coping with varied terrain.

Some horses appear to have a sixth sense which tells them exactly where to put their feet when they have absolutely no means of seeing where their feet are going down. They seem much more capable when allowed to lower the head, not only for drop fences but also when scrambling over rough or stony ground. This could have something to do with focussing vision in advance, or with sensing the going (some say the tactile hairs on the muzzle work like 'radar'), or possibly smell, although this option is least likely - there are so many scents to be detected at ground level that it is hard to imagine that one in particular could be associated with ground levels.

The most logical explanation for a lowered head carriage at a drop fence is to adjust the centre of balance. Before jumping down a step, a horse will both lower his head and start to buckle at the knees. Rather as we will bend and perhaps put a hand down to ground level before jumping down, the horse will get his weight down as much as possible to reduce the impact of landing and the risk of injury. As this happens, the centre of balance will be lower and further back towards the hind legs, assisting the horse in striding on afterwards without falling onto his forehand and possibly overbalancing.

FG

...and then an easy
jump down and out..

43

HOW IMPORTANT ARE THE
senses of smell and taste to horses?

Horses use their senses, including those of smell and taste, in a variety of ways to pick up all sorts of messages.

The sense of smell is important to the horse for exploring its environment, identifying feeding material and in group and individual recognition. The horse's long nasal passages allow it, through sniffing actions, to intensify odours, thus enabling it to detect odour molecules.

In addition the horse's vomeronasal organ, situated on the floor of the nasal cavity, detects pheromones. Pheromones are chemicals that are used to transmit information such as the reproductive state of an animal, the emotional state and so on. This is why it is said that horses (and dogs) can 'smell' fear in humans. Through the behaviour, called Flehmen, in which the horse apparently curls its top lip to allow the air to 'drop' on to the vomeronasal organ, additional screening for the information-transmitting pheromones can take place. This is often seen performed by the stallion during mating, and is often misinterpreted by horse owners as the horse appearing to laugh! Taste and smell are intricately interwoven, and so must be considered together. Although, as with most mammals, horses have taste buds on their tongue, it is not known whether horses have a particularly acute sense of taste. Since food selection must involve the sense of taste, and many studies have shown that horses do have certain food preferences, it seems likely that they discriminate between items of food on the basis of taste and smell.

Horses have very long nasal passages.

44

The Flehmen response is used to detect pheromones.

Taste and smell are also important in communication. Horses scent mark, via faeces piles such as those used by stallions to announce their presence, they deposit the group smell over their bodies through the use of communal rolling areas, and they use scent to recognise their young.

NW

CAN HORSES
actually feel happy?

Horses can - and do - feel happy, but it takes a good horseman or horsewoman to be able to identify this emotion.

When it comes to the equine mind, I think we have to be very clear as to what constitutes contentment and what shows itself as happiness - for there is a big difference. A horse may well be content with good husbandry, a comfy clean stable and plentiful food. To be happy requires rather more than material comforts, and I believe this has to start with a partnership since real happiness is generally all about the state of the horse in his work.

There is no doubt that equine happiness will shine out for all to see, but perhaps one has to be a horseman or horsewoman to recognise it. I am often amazed how some (even quite knowledgeable) people mistake tension for happiness. For example, standing beside a jump, a horse soars over and bounds onward for the next one. It is all over so quickly, it is hard to tell whether the horse is really happy or not, since willingness to serve is not always a sign of happiness. Often horses do things for us, despite their fear, apprehension or the fact they actually would much prefer to do something else!

Take dressage, for example. While some horses love the discipline, it is sad to say that for many it is a complete turn-off. I blame a lack of education for this since too many people take up dressage without having sufficient knowledge to know how to make it fun or comfortable for their horse as well as educational. People are also naive about the outward signs of happiness as, for example, in a superb display of top level dressage where the horse's muscles may be bulging, the steps high and elevated and the ears sharply pricked forward. Often onlookers immediately assume the horse is really enjoying himself because it all looks so wonderful. Sometimes, the contrary is in fact the case.

Equine happiness will shine out for all to see if you look for the signs.

47

One has first to recognise that good, even stunning, performance is not necessarily linked to happiness. Whilst a tense horse may look more impressive, with every muscle straining and the veins standing out as we so often see in equestrian photographs, a happy horse will look altogether softer through relaxation of mind and body. Whilst some muscles will tense, it has to be remembered that others will stretch so the whole appearance should be flowing with a certain looseness which is never present in the tense, unhappy horse. As for the steps, horses can be made to do extravagant steps whether happy or otherwise; it is all a matter of how fit and to how high a level they have been trained, so that alone is no indication.

It is the state of the horse's neck and head however which gives away the clearest signs of the state of mind. It is often said that a horse's mouth is the 'barometer' of the soul. A supple jaw coupled with a relaxed, 'happy' mouth will be moist and may even produce a great deal of foam. Many people mistakenly think this is a sign of stress, but generally it shows a horse correctly chewing on the bit, relaxing the poll and stretching and rounding the neck, with the spine articulating correctly and without resistance.

Another telltale sign of a happy horse is the state of the ears which should be attentive but never fixed. Completely floppy ears often indicate over-submission, whereas the ears of a happy horse should frequently turn back to the rider with the horse listening in every stride. This is very different from ears laid back as a precursor to a kick or a bite.

For me personally, the best sign of all that I have got it right is when the horse blows down his nose in an audible, 'whoofly' sort of way as he is working. This is nothing to do with heavy breathing or poor wind. It is the noise that is produced by a horse that is in absolute rhythm with his own body and in equal partnership with his rider. It is displayed mostly in canter, and in one particular stallion of mine, we only hear this noise when his back is up, he is light in the hand and he is really swinging through in the gait. It is lovely - and must be music in the ears to all who love horses!

A happy horse will look relaxed in mind and body.

Finally, I think horses, like human beings, need a regular input of love to realise their full happiness potential. Love is something that has to be unconditional for horses to be touched by it. The amazing thing about horses is that you can't kid them; they somehow know when they are truly loved and will blossom accordingly.

SL

WHY DO HORSES

pick up their forefeet whilst eating?

Many horses do this but, interestingly, it's a type of behaviour associated more with short feeds, not hay and grazing.

Many, but certainly not all, horses dig or wave their forefeet when they are eating. They will do this at the door in anticipation of a feed as well. Some just hold a foreleg flexed up, with the hoof near to the elbow. Some stamp, others dig. Some horses are very restrained, others quite violent. The interesting point is that this type of behaviour is almost always exhibited with short feed, not hay or grazing.

To answer why horses do this, we need to look at when this behaviour might be exhibited in natural circumstances.

When the ground is covered in snow, the only way a grazing horse can get to the grass is to clear the snow away with its fore hoof. It may have to dig quite hard with the toe to break through hard ice or frost, then scrape the snow back. In some arid areas, it is possible that horses might reach water by digging a hole.

A young or inquisitive horse will use its forefeet to investigate strange objects. A horse which dislikes its presence can even attack a dog or fox. Horses will dig at favoured bits of ground that may contain certain minerals, or something else unknown that takes their taste. Horses also dig before rolling and as an expression of pain, such as colic.

So, why do they adapt this natural behaviour to feed time? Several of the natural situations involving digging are associated with the horse needing more. It is hungry, greedy or thirsty. The manger feed is a very artificial feed for a horse. It is only available occasionally. It contains cereals, which are starchy, tasty, and unavailable in natural circumstances. Additionally, the feed is likely to be molassed, which makes it even tastier. The horse cannot get this wonderful food down quickly enough! Although not particularly hungry or starved, its very nature makes the horse greedy for it, in the same way as children can be greedy for sweet food.

JVL

OW WOULD A DOMESTICATED HORSE COPE IF
returned the wild?

There are many examples of domesticated horses which have been released, both accidentally and deliberately. Horses can, given the right conditions and preparation, re-establish themselves in a herd in the wild.

Horses have been domesticated for around 5,000 years. During that time, the very many different breeds have been developed, and specialised skills such as racing speed and draught power have been bred into different types. A lot, you may think, has been achieved in those few millennia. But against that, we must remember that the horse has been evolving on its own for around 50 million years. Domesticity can only be a thin veneer over a creature so successful in its development.

So, how would a domesticated horse cope on returning to the wild? This is not a new concept and has in fact been achieved with complete success at various times in history.

The majority of our native breeds are not in fact wild, but feral. This means that they have at one time been domesticated, then have been released (or escaped) back into the wild. Those free-living herds, which still remain, are undoubtedly successful. The most successful, however, are probably the Exmoor ponies, which cope so well with the extreme conditions on their native heath; there is good evidence to suppose that these may in fact be truly wild.

The Brumbies of Australia and the Mustangs of America are good examples of domesticated horses which have reclaimed their wild, atavistic roots. So successful are these herds that they have created a nuisance in some areas and extensive, controversial culling programmes are employed in an attempt to control their numbers. The success of these horses must be due in some part to the fact that they are in areas ideal for horses: open countryside and grasslands.

Coming closer to the present, there have been successful attempts to return zoo-bred Mongolian Wild Horses to a free-living life-style, both on the Steppes of Central Eurasia and on a smaller scale, in a remote area of France. There are many examples of domesticated horses being released, both accidentally and deliberately, and it is suggested that within a period of five years, any domesticated horse will have successfully re-established in a wild herd, both socially and physically.

A very pampered domesticated horse, which has been stabled and rugged in the winter, will need two or three years without rugging to become accustomed to growing a sufficient winter coat. If it had been just chucked out on to a prairie somewhere, it is possible it would not survive this adaptive period. Similarly, if it was not accustomed to being with other horses, and did not understand the social niceties of equine behaviour, it could become isolated or victimised, which would not help its survival.

But in the end, the influence of 50 million years of evolution must have a stronger influence than 5,000 years of domesticity. Beneath that well-groomed, benevolent exterior, there lurks a wild animal waiting its chance to flee back to the freedom and comfort of its herd.

JVL

> The influence of 50 million years of evolution must have a stronger influence than 5,000 years of domesticity.

CAN A HORSE
find its way home?

Many horses seem to have a natural homing instinct, although others need human help to steer them in the right direction. What 'pulls' or draws them to home is open to debate.

We always fondly like to imagine that horses have some extra magical powers that will help us if we get into trouble - such as getting lost, particularly in the dark or fog! Some owners, and fiction writers, tell amazing stories about horses' abilities in this respect. In real life, the truth can be rather different. My experience is that many horses are pretty useless at this, but a few are brilliant...

I recall one ride on my old mare, Sarah. We got lost on a late autumn afternoon. I hacked us both in what felt like a large circle but found, to my horror, that I was in a village miles from where I thought we were.

A farmer told me that the safest way home, in view of the approaching darkness, was to turn round and go back the way we had come down lighted roads as before us were only dark lanes and tracks. Once turned, the mare took charge, seeming highly relieved, and set off in a determined, spanking trot. I gave her her head.

She plainly knew the straight-line direction home and seemed to be using her head like a compass needle, slightly turned towards 'magnetic north' (home) no matter in which direction we were facing on the winding roads.

Some zoologists think that mammals and birds can follow the earth's magnetic fields.

Zoologists studying migrating mammals and birds now feel that they do, in fact, follow the earth's magnetic fields, which most humans cannot detect.

Every time we reached a crossroads, Sarah unerringly took the correct turn without waiting for me to ponder which way to go. Each time we reached an open gate she tried to turn in, obviously planning to gallop home across country in a dead straight line, no matter what! A brilliant jumper, I knew she could do it, old as she was, and horses see much better than humans in the dark, anyway - but I didn't have the nerve!

Once home she wanted no thanks: with me still on top, she dived into her open box door and did the longest pee I ever knew her to do!
SMcB

DO HORSES
mourn the loss of a friend?

Because horses do not always make their feelings very clear, we have to be ultra-sensitive to the signals they do give us. When they suffer a loss, they will not react in the way that humans would...

Horses do not weep, whine or sob. They do not have a howl of pain. But just because they do not use expressions of physical or emotional hurt that we are familiar with, it is not to say that they do not suffer.

When we suffer a great loss, not only might we weep, but we will also feel depressed and miserable. We may not want to eat. We probably won't feel like going out or socialising. We might want to sit quietly in places we shared with our lost one, and we could spend time just thinking about our missed friend, reminiscing on times past. Other than shedding tears, horses can be observed doing all these things, but we do not always see them for what they are.

Horses are naturally herd animals. Within the loose association of the herd, however, they will have strong bonds with particular individuals. The 'best friend' is quite often a close relation in a family-based herd, but can be even a different breed. Can a horse mourn the loss of this best friend? The best way to examine this is for me to relate an actual example.

My own herd of Arab horses is very stable. They are all settled, know their place and function in the group and rarely have disagreements. They are all related. Tinks and Chrissy were born nine days apart. They had the same sire, and their dams were aunt and niece to each other, so they were very closely related. They were also both bay. They played and grew up together. As time went on, they became best friends. They would hang out together, mutually groom and go for mad dashes together. When I was moving from the farm in Essex to the present farm in Suffolk, they went together to my sister's yard for four months while I was sorting things out. If one was ridden and the other left behind, it did not matter. They were not worried, but pleased to see one another when they got back.

Time went on and they moved to my new yard. Tinks was a good girl and easy to catch, so her schooling progressed and soon she found a new home. Chrissy was a bit of a wild child and would only be caught if there were several coming in, so her schooling did not progress. So Tinks moved on and Chrissy stayed. She did not gallop around whinnying or try to jump over the fence when her best friend went. She looked perfectly all right, and anyway, she had the rest of the herd with her.

But was she upset, really? She was often on her own, with the herd, yes, but not close to any particular horse. She was rarely seen mutually grooming (which she had loved to do with Tinks). To catch her now meant that every one else had to be caught first. She seemed withdrawn. Her schooling ceased. She looked well and normal, but I am sure, in retrospect, that she missed her friend.

By chance, after a couple of years and still not developing any really close bond, a friend asked if I knew of a nice little mare looking for a home. My wild child was in luck! Chrissy was boxed up and taken, sweating and screaming, to her new home. Not one member of her herd acknowledged that she was going or even bothered to return her neighs. At her new home, she had lots of personal attention, two other Arabs and a funny little skewbald pony for company. Contrary to all expectations, she fell in love with the old pony and after two years, now has a best friend again. They are never far apart and do all the things that she used to do with Tinks. Chrissy is brighter in herself, more confident and much easier to catch. She is even whinnying to Sharon's husband, much to his delight.

Was she mourning the loss of Tinks? With hindsight, I'd say most certainly, but without words. We have to be so sensitive to the other signals horses give us. All too often, we do not read them.
JVL

WHAT CAUSES 'vices'?

Boredom was traditionally given as the main cause of so-called vices. However, there are other ways in which we need to look at these problems, including inheritance.

Vices in horse are those annoying or even damaging habits horses sometimes develop, especially when they are stabled for extensive periods, isolated from their friends or given an inappropriate diet. Weaving, crib-biting, wind-sucking and box-walking are probably the best known. Others include rug-tearing, door- or wall-kicking and flanking. Flanking is a form of self-mutilation, usually performed by stallions or colts and involves the horse biting itself, often accompanied by running round in small circles.

The usual reaction to a stable vice in a horse is to condemn the horse as a nutter, and restrict its environment even more (bars at the door, hours spent being tied up, further isolation to stop others 'catching' the habit). Curiously, if a zoo animal develops a similar stereotypic behaviour, everyone immediately condemns the zoo for keeping it in a 'cruel' way; likewise, tigers pacing their cage in a circus. Odd behaviours in pets are explained as being due to having been taken away from its mother too soon. But very few people look at horses' vices as a result of any form of human failing to respond adequately to those horses' needs.

Crib-biting is one of the more common stable 'vices'.

So, what then actually causes these problems in horse? Boredom has traditionally been cited as the cause, but I think this can now be excluded. The underlying factor is probably genetic. The horse inherits (or not) the tendency to develop a 'vice' if the environment triggers it. The trigger is usually in the form of stress, or distress even. Horses need company, space and continuous supplies of relatively low grade feed in the form of grazing. Deny any of these to a susceptible individual, and a vice will result.

Weavers and box walkers, for instance, are often active, alert horses

that like to be on the move. They are bright, busy types for whom isolation in a small space is complete anathema. Several endurance horses of my acquaintance weave or box walk. Their sport suits them well; confinement does not.

The role of genetics is often misunderstood and usually underestimated, but as a breeder of horses, it is never unexpected when one sees behavioural or psychological traits passing from one generation to another. I have a long line of one branch of my horse family that all chase dogs with an apparently genuine loathing. Three generations of another line produced weavers, in spite of providing what most people would consider a wholly suitable environment, albeit with some stabling every day. Even the way a horse tosses its head can be identical to that of its sire, never seen. Although one cannot say that weaving or cribbing is directly inherited, it is possible to say that these aberrations are more likely in some families than others. The tendency to react to adverse conditions in a certain way is programmed into the genes. All that is then needed is the environmental trigger.

Elephants, apparently, 'weave' to maintain their blood circulation and body heat. Perhaps there is some factor in horses' evolution that could make some of these behaviour patterns advantageous. Whatever it is, I do not believe any of us likes to see any horse frantically repeating some seemingly useless behaviour pattern over and over. In the end, it is a sign that we have failed the horse.
JVL

DO HORSES NEED
to sleep?

The way in which we manage and care for horses has an effect on their rest and sleep patterns, both of which are important for physical and mental wellbeing.

Having inactive periods during the day is as important to the horse as it is to us. Rest and sleep enable the body and brain to have time to repair and reorganise themselves. The horse shows various forms of inactivity, such as idling, drowsing and sleeping.

The nature of sleep in horses has been looked at by researchers and they have found that horses show both slow wave (deep) sleep and rapid eye movement (paradoxical) sleep. On average it has been shown that mature horses spend up to 2.4 hours per day drowsing and 3.4 hours per day actually sleeping. Most of this occurs at night, especially sleeping.

Although horses lie down for a total of approximately 2.5 hours per day, this is usually broken up into shorter periods. Horses will lie down on their sternum, but also laterally. However mature horses usually limit lateral lying to very short periods due to the pressure this places upon their respiratory system, and the fact that when asleep in this position they are extremely vulnerable to danger! Young horses do tend to rest and sleep more than older ones, and of course there is a fair amount of individual variation too. It is also the case that not all sleeping and resting happen when the horse is lying down. Horses have a unique stay mechanism in their hindlegs, which allows them to drowse, and possibly sleep, standing up.

As with all other horse behaviour, management regimes do have an effect on the horse's rest and sleep patterns. If a horse is taken to a new environment, such as being stabled overnight at a show, it is unlikely to lie down or to sleep well. In fact, horses that are moved to new homes may experience reduced sleep for a period of up to a month! In addition, long distance transport, or being placed somewhere where it is physically impossible to relax or lie down, will reduce sleep.

This has important consequences - just as it does for humans. It is likely that sleep-deprived horses are most likely to be affected by stress-related illnesses, and certainly are likely to suffer a reduction in performance, too. For example it is known that learning can be hindered by depriving an animal of lying down in REM (rapid eye movement) sleep. This may be because the horse needs this time to ensure storage of new information in long term memory. Thus, there is certainly something to be said for letting sleeping horses lie!

NW

Inactive periods during the day are important for horses.

DO HORSES HAVE
extra sensory perception?

This is a question we will never know the answer to for certain, but horsemen and women the world over have strong views on the ESP capabilities of horses...

Horses often give every impression of possessing an extra-sensory perception of life that we humans usually do not have. An example of this, from many years ago, which always sticks in my mind involved two firm equine friends, one of which had to be taken to a veterinary hospital for a minor operation.

The box came to take the mare away at 11 am, her gelding friend having to be shut in his box with the top door closed to prevent him trying to follow. He was most distressed, pacing his box, calling and sweating, until about 1 pm when he suddenly calmed down but appeared sad. At about 4 pm he started again pacing and shouting, continuing until the mare returned late that night.

It was concluded that, as long as both horses were conscious they were in communication with each other, but that as soon as the mare's anaesthetic took effect at around 1 pm this link was broken so she was no longer able to communicate, distantly, to her gelding friend her distress at being away from home and him. When she came round, she once again 'told' him she was worried and upset so he, too, became agitated until the two were reunited. Half an hour before the box appeared in the yard, the gelding calmed down and looked expectantly down the drive, long before he could have heard or smelled it. It is very hard to explain this by any other means than extra-sensory perception.

This brings me to the work being done by Dr Rupert Sheldrake on morphic fields in animals, in which an animal knows long before it could have any physical warning when an owner is coming home. I know of a pony called Freddie, who is owned by Mrs Olwen Way,

Horses sometimes stand stock still with heads up and ears pricked, gazing into the distance, impervious to any efforts of their handlers to get them moving on.

61

Secretary of The Equine Behaviour Forum, and who always knows long before she arrives at her son's house to feed him (at purposely erratic times) that she is on the way. My own first horse also knew long before I arrived at his livery yard when I was coming to see him.

Horses sometimes stand stock still with heads up and ears pricked, gazing into the distance, absolutely impervious to any efforts of their riders or handlers to get them moving on. Scientists call this state 'catatonic immobility' but always describe it as a state of extreme fear in the animal concerned: it seems paralysed with fear (presumably a primitive way of becoming invisible to a predator), but I have found no definite evidence of this state in horses which, of course, are prey animals not prone to freezing to the spot but to galloping off at top speed.

Members of the Equine Behaviour Forum reported this state in their horses (and my first horse did it often, but no others have done so), all stressed that their horses seemed quite calm and relaxed but 'in another world'. Many members put this down to extra-sensory perception, as though their horse were receiving information from another dimension. However, as horses' senses are different from, and much more acute than, ours it seems more appropriate, perhaps, to call it super-sensory perception. Horses can hear sound wavelengths above and below those we can detect, and my feeling is that the horses often hear something fascinating that our hearing cannot pick up.

There are many reported instances of apparent extra-sensory perception which scientists would call 'anecdotal evidence': they are not scientifically documented or proven, and therefore unacceptable as scientific evidence - which, of course, does not mean that they are not true.

A case in point is horses refusing to pass so-called haunted places. There have been many instances over thousands of years of reported ghostly sightings and happenings, and scientific investigations into them, without any satisfactory scientific proof resulting.

It seems that animals do pick up on such things. A friend of mine bought a horse which refused consistently to pass a house which it was 'known' had a poltergeist in it. When my friend bought the horse and moved him into his livery yard, they were both new to the area and she, too, did not know about the poltergeist, so this cannot be explained away by saying that the rider was passing on 'fear vibes' to the horse.

SMcB

CAN HORSES
see in colour?

Until recently, it was felt that horses were not able to see the full spectrum of colours. Although there is still disagreement amongst researchers on horses' colour vision, there is little doubt that horses can distinguish between some colours.

The horse's retina consists of cells called cones, which are associated with colour vision. Earlier research suggested that horses were dichromates, with limited colour vision in the red-blue colour spectrum. The advantages to the horse of this sort of colour vision are not immediately apparent, since in a world where the horse's normal food is generally of shades of green (a mix of yellow and blue light), it might be expected these sort of cones would be more useful.

However there appears to be some disagreement between researchers in the colour-seeing abilities of horses, and recent research has indicated that horses can discriminate the colours red, yellow, green and blue from various shades of grey. This suggests that horses may have trichromatic colour vision, ie red, blue and yellow.

This disagreement between researchers may be because of the ways in which colour vision has been tested. Horses are usually trained to discriminate between different colours for a food reward, and the different conditions used by researchers conducting slightly different tests may have varied. Factors such as the amount of light available are likely to influence the results of the tests. Despite these differences of opinion, there seems no doubt that horses can distinguish between some colours.

Anecdotal evidence suggests that mares do use colour markings as well as smell to recognise their foals, and some horses do appear to have a preference for a certain colour of horse. This is especially obvious in stallions, who sometimes respond better to mares of a certain colour.

NW

INDEX